To Rose

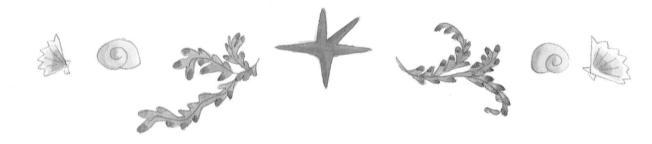

A Thousand Yards of Sea

A Collection of Sea Stories and Poems

Compiled by Laura Cecil

Pictures by Emma Chichester Clark

Greenwillow Books, New York

Library of Congress Cataloging-in-Publication Data
A Thousand yards of sea : a collection of sea stories and poems /
compiled by Laura Cecil ; pictures by Emma Chichester Clark.
p.   cm.
Summary: A collection of sea stories and poems by such authors
as Edward Lear, Margaret Mahy, and Rudyard Kipling.
ISBN 0-688-11437-7
1. Ocean—Literary collections.   [1. Ocean—Literary collections.
2. Sea stories.]   I. Cecil, Laura.   II. Chichester Clark, Emma ill.
PZ5.T373 1993 808.8′032162—dc20 91-35687 CIP AC

ACKNOWLEDGMENTS

Thanks are due to the following for permission to reprint copyright material:

"The Man Whose Mother Was a Pirate" from *The Man Whose Mother Was a Pirate* by Margaret Mahy (J.M. Dent and Sons Ltd.), copyright © 1972 by Margaret Mahy. Reprinted by permission of J.M. Dent and Sons Ltd. and Helen Hoke Ltd.

"The Underwater Wibbles" from *The New Kid on the Block* by Jack Prelutsky (Greenwillow Books), copyright © 1984 by Jack Prelutsky. Reprinted by permission of Greenwillow Books (a division of William Morrow and Company Inc., New York) and William Heinemann Ltd. (a part of Reed International Books Ltd., London).

"A Thousand Yards of Sea" by Adèle Geras, first printed in *Cricket Magazine*, copyright © 1976 by Adèle Geras. Reprinted by permission of the author.

"Fishes' Evening Song" from *Whisperings and Other Things* by Dahlov Ipcar (Alfred A. Knopf), copyright © 1967 by Dahlov Ipcar. Reprinted by permission of McIntosh and Otis, Inc.

"The Green Kitten" from *Jim at the Corner* by Eleanor Farjeon (Oxford University Press), copyright © 1958 by Gervase Farjeon. Reprinted by permission of David Higham Associates Ltd., London.

"O'er Seas that Have No Beaches" from *A Book of Nonsense* by Mervyn Peake (Peter Owen Ltd.), copyright © 1972 by Maeve Gilmore. Reprinted by permission of Peter Owen Ltd.

"Jonah and the Whale and the Cod-Liver Oil" from *Pohádky* by Miloš Macourek (Artia, Czechoslovakia). Reprinted by permission of Miloš Macourek. English translation copyright © 1980 by Marie Burg. Reprinted by permission of Marie Burg.

"A Sea Story" from *The Wonder Dog* by Richard Hughes (Chatto and Windus), copyright © 1977 by Richard Hughes. Reprinted by permission of David Higham Associates Ltd., London.

"Little Fan" from *The Wandering Moon and Other Poems* by James Reeves (Puffin Books), copyright © 1950 by James Reeves. Reprinted by permission of the James Reeves Estate.

"Prince Crab" retold from *Il Principe Granchio*, Volume 3, Number 10, collected by Bernoni (Venice). Retelling copyright © 1992 by Laura Cecil.

Every effort has been made to trace all the copyright holders, and the Publishers apologize if any inadvertent omission has been made.

Contents

The Jumblies

Edward Lear

They went to sea in a Sieve, they did,
    In a Sieve they went to sea:
In spite of all their friends could say,
On a winter's morn, on a stormy day,
    In a Sieve they went to sea!
And when the Sieve turned round and round,
And every one cried, "You'll all be drowned!"
They called aloud, "Our Sieve ain't big,
But we don't care a button! we don't care a fig!
    In a Sieve we'll go to sea!"
      Far and few, far and few,
        Are the lands where the Jumblies live;
        Their heads are green, and their hands are blue,
        And they went to sea in a Sieve.

They sailed away in a Sieve, they did,
  In a Sieve they sailed so fast,
With only a beautiful pea-green veil
Tied with a riband by way of a sail,
  To a small tobacco-pipe mast;
And every one said, who saw them go,
"O won't they be soon upset, you know!
For the sky is dark, and the voyage is long,
And happen what may, it's extremely wrong
  In a Sieve to sail so fast!"
    Far and few, far and few,
      Are the lands where the Jumblies live;
      Their heads are green, and their hands are blue,
      And they went to sea in a Sieve.

The water it soon came in, it did,
    The water it soon came in;
So to keep them dry, they wrapped their feet
In a pinky paper all folded neat,
    And they fastened it down with a pin.
And they passed the night in a crockery-jar,
And each of them said, "How wise we are!
Though the sky be dark, and the voyage be long,
Yet we never can think we were rash or wrong,
    While round in our Sieve we spin!"
      Far and few, far and few,
        Are the lands where the Jumblies live;
      Their heads are green, and their hands are blue,
        And they went to sea in a Sieve.

And all night long they sailed away;
    And when the sun went down,
They whistled and warbled a moony song
To the echoing sound of a coppery gong,
    In the shade of the mountains brown.
"O Timballo! How happy we are,
When we live in a sieve and a crockery-jar,
And all night long in the moonlight pale,
We sail away with a pea-green sail,
    In the shade of the mountains brown!"
        Far and few, far and few,
            Are the lands where the Jumblies live;
            Their heads are green, and their hands are blue,
            And they went to sea in a Sieve.

They sailed to the Western Sea, they did,
　　To a land all covered with trees,
And they bought an Owl, and a useful Cart,
And a pound of Rice, and a Cranberry Tart,
　　And a hive of silvery Bees.
And they bought a Pig, and some green Jack-daws,
And a lovely Monkey with lollipop paws,
And forty bottles of Ring-Bo-Ree,
　　And no end of Stilton Cheese.
　　　Far and few, far and few,
　　　　Are the lands where the Jumblies live;
　　　Their heads are green, and their hands are blue,
　　　　And they went to sea in a Sieve.

12

And in twenty years they all came back,
　　In twenty years or more,
And every one said, "How tall they've grown!
For they've been to the Lakes, and the Torrible Zone,
　　And the hills of the Chankly Bore."
And they drank their health, and gave them a feast
Of dumplings made of beautiful yeast;
And every one said, "If we only live,
We too will go to sea in a Sieve, —
　　To the hills of the Chankly Bore!"
　　　Far and few, far and few,
　　　　Are the lands where the Jumblies live;
　　　Their heads are green, and their hands are blue,
　　　　And they went to sea in a Sieve.

The Man Whose Mother Was a Pirate

Margaret Mahy

There was once a little man who had never seen the sea, although his mother was an old pirate woman. The two of them lived in a great city, far, far from the seashore.

The little man had a brown suit with black buttons, and a brown tie and shiny shoes — all most respectable and handsome. He worked in a neat office and wrote down rows of figures in books, and ruled lines under them. And before he spoke, he always coughed *"Hrrrrm!"*

Well, one day his mother said, "Shipmate, I want to see the sea again. I want to get the city smoke out of my lungs and put the sea salt there instead. I want to fire my old silver pistol off again, and see the waves jump in surprise."

"*Hrrrrm*, Mother," the little man said, very respectful and polite. "I haven't got a car or even a horse, and no money to get one or the other. All we have is a wheelbarrow and a kite."

"We must make do," his mother answered sharply. "I will go and load my silver pistol and polish my cutlass."

The little man went to work. He asked Mr Fat (who was the man he worked for), "*Hrrrrm*, Mr Fat! May I have two weeks to take my mother to the seaside?"

"I don't go to the seaside," Mr Fat snapped out. "Why should you need to go?"

"*Hrrrrm*, it is for my mother," the little man explained.

"I don't see why you should want to go to the seaside," said Mr Fat, crossly. "There is nothing there but water . . . salty at that! I once found a penny in the sand, but that is all the money I have ever made at the seaside. There is nothing financial about the sea."

"*Hrrrrm*, it is for my mother," the little man said again. "I will be back in two weeks."

"Make sure you are!" Mr Fat answered crossly.

★

So they set off, the little man pushing his mother in the wheelbarrow, and his mother holding the kite.

His mother's short gray hair ruffled merrily out under the green scarf she wore tied around her head. Her gold earrings challenged the sun, throwing his own light back to him. Between her lips was her old black pipe, and she wore, behind her ear, a rose that matched her scarlet shawl. The little man wore his brown suit and boots, all buttoned and tied. He trotted along, pushing the wheelbarrow.

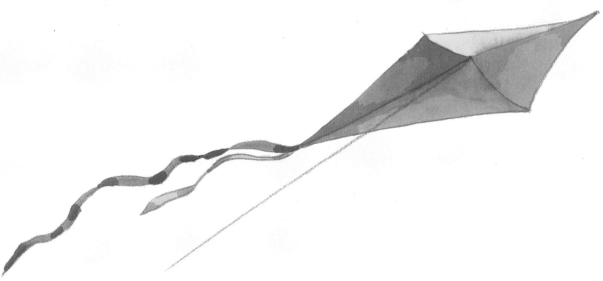

As they went, his mother talked about the sea. She told him of its voices:

"It sings at night with a sad booming voice. Under the sun it laughs and slaps the side of the ship in time to its laughter. Yes, and then, when a storm comes, it screams and hates poor sailors. And the sea is a great gossip! What is the weather at Tierra del Fuego? Is the ice moving in Hudson Bay? Where are the great whales sailing? The sea knows it all, and one wave mutters and whispers it to another, and to those who know how to listen."

"*Hrrrrm*, yes indeed, Mother," the little man said, pattering the wheelbarrow along. His shoes hurt rather.

"Where are you going?" a farming fellow asked him.

"*Hrrrrm*, I'm taking Mother to the seaside," the little man answered.

"I wouldn't go there," the farming fellow remarked. "It's not a safe place at all. It's wet and cold and gritty, I'm told . . . not comfortable like a cowshed."

"*Hrrrrm*, it's very musical, Mother says," the little man replied.

In his mind he heard the laughter and the boom and the scream and the song of the sea. He trotted along, pushing the wheelbarrow. His mother rested her chin on her knees as she jolted along.

"Yes, it is blue in the sunshine," she said. "And when the sun goes in, the sea becomes green. Yet in the twilight I have seen it gray and serene, and at night, inky-black and wild, it tosses beside the ship. Sunrise turns it to burning gold, the moon to liquid silver. There is always change in the sea."

They came to a river . . . There was no boat.

The little man tied the wheelbarrow, with his mother in it, to the kite string. His neat little moustache was wild and ruffled by the wind. Now he ran barefoot.

"*Hrrrrm!* Hold on tight, Mother," he called.

Up in the air they went as the wind took the kite with it. The little man dangled from the kite string and his mother swung in her wheelbarrow basket.

"This is all very well, Sam," she shouted to him, "but the sea — ah the sea! It rocks you to sleep, tosses you in the air, pulls you down to the deep. It speeds you along and holds you still. It storms you and calms you. The sea is bewitching but bewildering.

"*Hrrrrm,* yes, Mother," the little man said. As he dangled from the kite string he saw the sea in his mind — the blue and the green of it, the rise and the fall, the white wings of the birds, the white wings of the ships.

The kite let them down gently on the other side of the river.

"Where are you going?" asked a philosopher fellow who sat there.

"*Hrrrrm!* I'm taking Mother to the sea," the little man told him.

"Why do you want to go there?"

"*Hrrrm!* The sea is something very special," the little man answered him. "It is full of music and strange songs and stories, full of shadows and movement. My mother is very fond of it."

"You love it too, don't you, little man?" said the philosopher.

"Well," the little man replied, "the more I hear my mother talk about it, the more the thought of it swells inside me, all glowing and wonderful."

Then the philosopher shook his head. "Go back, go back, little man," he cried, "because the wonderful things are always less wonderful than you hope they will be . . . The sea is less warm, the joke less funny, the taste is not as good as the smell."

The old pirate mother called from the wheelbarrow, waving her cutlass.

"I must go," the little man said shyly.

Off he ran, and as he trundled his mother away, he noticed that two buttons had popped off his coat.

Something new came into the wind scent.

"Ah, there's the salt!" His mother sniffed the wind. "There's nothing as joyful as a salt-sea wind."

Suddenly they came over a hill . . . Suddenly there was the sea.

The little man could only stare. He hadn't dreamed of the BIGNESS of it, the blueness of it. He hadn't thought it would roll like kettledrums, and swish itself on to the beach. He heard the strange, wild music of waves and seabirds, and smelled wet sand and seaweed and fish and ropes and driftwood. The little man opened his eyes and his mouth, and the drift and the dream of it, the weave and the wave of it, the fume and the foam of it flooded into him and never left him again. At his feet the sea stroked the sand with soft little paws. Farther out the waves pounced and bounced like puppies. And out beyond, again and again, the great, graceful breakers moved like kings into court, trailing the sea like a peacock-patterned robe behind them.

Then, with joy, the little man and his mother danced hornpipes along the beach. How the little man's neat clothes grew wild and happy to be free.

A rosy sea captain came along. "Well, here are two likely people," the captain said. "Will you be my bo'sun, madam? And you, little man, can be the cabin-boy."

"*Hrrrrm*, thank you!" said the little man.

"Say 'Aye, aye, sir!'" roared the captain.

"Aye, aye, sir!" smartly replied the little man as if he had never had a "*Hrrrrm!*" in his throat. And then he sang as he twirled on his toes.

> *"No wonder that*
> *I dance on my toes.*
> *Goodbye Mr Fat*
> *And figures in rows,*
> *Figures in rows*
> *And ink's blue gleaming.*
> *For where the sea goes*
> *Is beyond all dreaming."*

So Sailor Sam went on to the ship with his pirate mother and the sea captain, and a year later somebody brought Mr Fat a letter that had been washed ashore in a bottle.

"Having a wonderful time," it read. "Why don't *you* run off to sea, too?"

And if you want to find any moral to this story, you must go to sea and find it.

The Underwater Wibbles

Jack Prelutsky

The Underwater Wibbles
dine exclusively on cheese,
they keep it in containers
which they bind about their knees,
they often chew on Cheddar
which they slice into a dish,
and gorge on Gorgonzola
to the wonder of the fish.

The Underwater Wibbles
wiggle blithely through the sea,
munching merrily on Muenster,
grated Feta, bits of Brie,
passing porpoises seem puzzled,
stolid octopuses stare,
as the Wibbles nibble Gouda,
Provolone, Camembert.

The Underwater Wibbles
frolic gaily off the coast,
eating melted Mozzarella
served on soggy crusts of toast,
Wibbles gobble Appenzeller
as they execute their dives,
oh, the Underwater Wibbles
live extraordinary lives.

A Thousand Yards of Sea

Adèle Geras

The fishing boat was rocking slowly in the blue waters
to and fro, to and fro. Tom Taffet the fisherman looked at the
heap of fish shining in the sun and thought, "What a lot I've
caught today! I shall haul in just one more catch and then make
for the harbor." He leaned over the edge of the little boat and
drew in his net. As he poured the fish onto the deck, sparks
of water slid from their pink-silvery, blue-silvery, brown-
speckled backs.

"There's a beauty," thought Tom. "I've never seen a fish
that color before." He picked it up by the tail to have a closer

look, and was so surprised that he sat down at once, right in the middle of his catch. He was holding the tail of a mermaid! Her hair was brown and hung with seaweed, her tail was mauve and blue and silver and green, and her eyes were the color of stormy water.

"Cod steaks and shrimp tails!" he said. "I thought mermaids lived only in stories and sea shanties. Am I dreaming?"

"Certainly not," said the mermaid. "I don't know who you are, but I'd be very grateful if you'd just put me back into the water. I was on my way home, you know."

"But I can't put you back," said Tom. "I could be rich if you would help me. We'd both be famous. I'd be able to buy a little house with a garden. I could grow flowers, and I'd never have to go fishing in the cold and the wind again."

"That sounds lovely for you," said the mermaid, "but I should hate it. I'd have to live in a glass box full of water and people would stare at me through the walls. I'd never see my family again."

"I would look after you as if you were my own daughter," said Tom. "You could live with me and my wife. We'd put your tank in the front room and I'd bring you wonderful toys and good things to eat."

"Would you like your daughter to live at the bottom of the sea?" asked the mermaid. "However many good things she had down there, wouldn't you miss her?" She began to cry. Tears like small pearls rolled down her cheeks and plopped onto the fish piled up on the deck.

The fisherman thought for a long time. His daughter was grown up with children of her own, but he could still remember how she used to cry when she was small. He would have hated to have her live at the bottom of the sea. He would have missed her very much.

"Oh, well," he sighed. "I suppose you're right. You are too young to leave home. It's a shame, that's what it is. No one will believe that I've seen you. They'll say I was dreaming."

"I'll give you something in return for setting me free," said the mermaid, smiling now. "And maybe they'll believe you after all. May I borrow your knife?"

"It's very sharp. Please be careful," said Tom. He picked up the mermaid and slipped her gently into the water. Then he put his knife in her hand. With a flash of her tail, she was gone.

"That's that then," said Tom to himself. "No mermaid and no knife. What a fool I am! Maybe I was dreaming, but my knife is gone and that's a pity. I shall have to buy a new one in the market tomorrow." He turned the little boat toward the harbor. It was night-time now and Tom could see the reflection of the stars dancing in the black water.

Suddenly he heard a voice say: "Please don't go so quickly. I'm carrying something very heavy." It was the mermaid. Tom was so surprised that he spilled a mug of cocoa all over his boots.

"Fish cakes and fillets!" he said. "I never thought to see you again. What's that you're holding?"

"It's a thousand yards of sea. I've rolled it up and tied it neatly. I'm sure on land people would like to buy some.

And here's your knife too." She pushed the bundle of sea into the boat, and handed the knife to Tom.

"Thank you very much, little mermaid," said Tom. He could not imagine what people were going to do with a length of water, but the mermaid was gone, so he could not ask her.

The next day, Tom went to market to try and sell a few yards of sea. He set the bundle on a big wooden box and cut the ropes of seaweed that the mermaid had tied so carefully. Wave upon wave of blue and green and silver fell around his feet. The colors shone and shifted and merged into one another.

"Come and buy! Come and buy! Genuine yards of sea, cut by a mermaid, yes a mermaid, just for me," he shouted.

"Guaranteed to bring luck! Lovely colors! Come and see the lovely colors."

People gathered around Tom's box and the women began to buy the silky, whispery stuff. At the end of the day, Tom Taffet had made enough money to buy a little house with a garden to grow flowers in.

The women made the yards of sea into dresses and petticoats that sounded like rushing water when they moved. And they called it taffeta, after Tom Taffet who brought it to the shore.

Fishes' Evening Song

Dahlov Ipcar

Flip flop,
Flip flap,
Slip slap,
Lip lap;
Water sounds,
Soothing sounds.
We fan our fins
As we lie
Resting here
Eye to eye.
Water falls
Drop by drop,
Plip plop,

Drip drop,
Plink plunk,
Splash splish;
Fish fins fan,
Fish tails swish,
Swush, swash, swish.
This we wish . . .
Water cold,
Water clear,
Water smooth,
Just to soothe
Sleepy fish.

The Green Kitten

Eleanor Farjeon

When I was a boy, I felt the call of the sea and ran away from the farm in Kent where I was born. Our farm was not far from the coast, and soon I came to Pegwell Bay, where the good ship *Rocking-horse* was riding at anchor.

The Captain saw me coming, through his telescope, and when I was near enough he called, "Come here, boy!" He had a commanding sort of voice, so I came.

He looked me up and down, and said, "My cabin-boy has just run away to go on a farm."

"That's funny," I said, "because I've just run away from a farm to go for a cabin-boy."

The Captain looked me up and down, and said, "You'll do. What's your name?"

"Jim," I said. "What's yours?"

"Cap'n Potts," he said. "Well Jim, we don't sail till tomorrow, and tonight I feel like shrimps."

"Like shrimps?" I said.

"Yes, like shrimps," said Cap'n Potts.

Now when he said he was feeling like shrimps, I thought Cap'n Potts meant he was feeling sad, or seedy, or something like that. But it turned out he meant just what he said, for he handed me a big shrimping-net, and said, "Go and catch some."

That was a job any boy would enjoy, be he cabin-boy or farm-boy. I kicked off my boots in a jiffy, and went shrimping among the pools on the beach. The pools were surrounded by rocks, and the rocks were covered with thick green weed, like wet hair, very slippery to the feet.

When I'd got a nice netful of shrimps, I took them aboard the *Rocking-horse* and Cap'n Potts said, "Well done, Jim! You'll make a first-class cabin-boy, I see. Take them below to Cookie, and tell him to boil them for tea."

I went below and found Cookie, and said, "Please, I'm Jim the new cabin-boy, please, and please, Cap'n Potts says will you please cook these shrimps for tea?"

"Shrimps!" said Cookie. "Do you call *this* a shrimp?"

He plunged his hand into the net, and fetched up what looked like a little lump of rock smothered in green seaweed. But the little lump wriggled in Cookie's hand, the little lump arched its weedy green back, the little lump waved a weedy green tail, the little lump pricked up two weedy green ears, the little lump wrinkled its weedy green nose and *spat*. Next thing, it jumped out of Cookie's big hands, and clawed its way up to my shoulder, where it sat rubbing its soft green head against my cheek.

The little lump was nothing less than a wee green Kitten, with eyes as pink as coral.

The next day, when *we* sailed, the Kitten sailed too, and before long it was the pet of the ship. But I was its favorite, and it always slept in my cabin. Being the cabin-boy, I had of course, a cabin to myself.

Now that first trip of mine we did not seem to have the best of luck. Everything the ship could have the *Rocking-horse* had, like a child who has chickenpox, measles and mumps, one after the other. The *Rocking-horse* had hurricanes, and icebergs, and pirates, and thunderbolts. Once she was wrecked, and once she was becalmed.

It was when she was becalmed that *my* adventure happened.

Cap'n Potts was a restless man, and liked to be on the move. It gave him the fidgets when the ship got stuck like that in the middle of the sea, and one evening he came up to me and said, "Jim, I feel like lobsters!"

"Never mind, Cap'n," I said. "Perhaps we'll get a move on tomorrow."

"Perhaps we will," said Cap'n Potts, "and perhaps we won't. But whether we do or don't, tonight I feel like lobsters." Then he handed me a lobster-pot, and said, "Go and catch some."

Then I saw what he meant, and I got into a diving-suit, tucked the lobster-pot under my arm, dived over the side of the *Rocking-horse*, and sank to the bottom.

There was I, just a little nipper, all alone on the bed of the ocean. And there I saw wonders, to be sure! Coral and pearl and golden sands, colored seaweed as big as bushes,

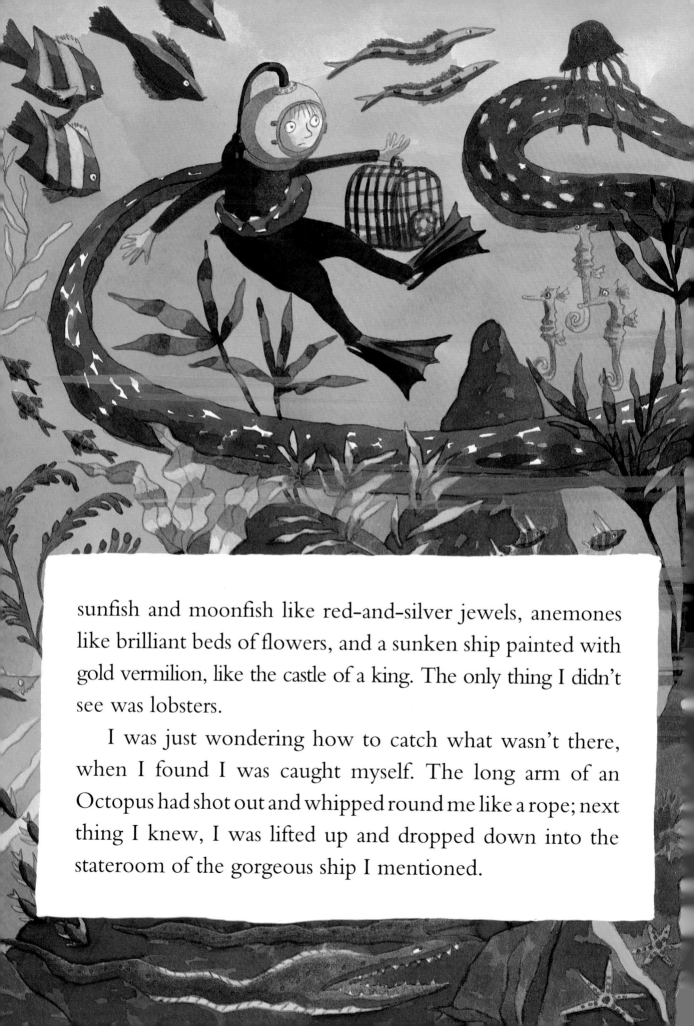

sunfish and moonfish like red-and-silver jewels, anemones like brilliant beds of flowers, and a sunken ship painted with gold vermilion, like the castle of a king. The only thing I didn't see was lobsters.

I was just wondering how to catch what wasn't there, when I found I was caught myself. The long arm of an Octopus had shot out and whipped round me like a rope; next thing I knew, I was lifted up and dropped down into the stateroom of the gorgeous ship I mentioned.

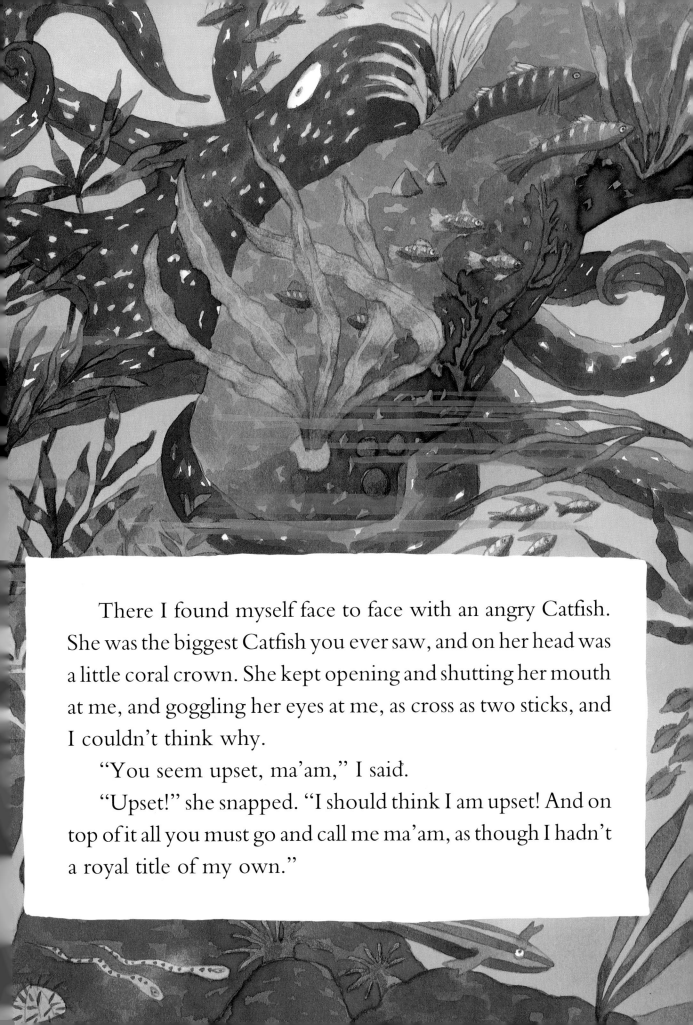

There I found myself face to face with an angry Catfish. She was the biggest Catfish you ever saw, and on her head was a little coral crown. She kept opening and shutting her mouth at me, and goggling her eyes at me, as cross as two sticks, and I couldn't think why.

"You seem upset, ma'am," I said.

"Upset!" she snapped. "I should think I am upset! And on top of it all you must go and call me ma'am, as though I hadn't a royal title of my own."

"Tell me what it is, and I'll call you by it, ma'am," said I.

"There you go again!" she snapped. "Where are your eyes, boy? Can't you see the crown on my head? I am the Queen of the Catfish, and I want my Kitten!"

"Your Kitten, ma'am-your-majesty?" said I.

"My Kitten, booby," she said, "that you caught in your shrimping-net. And till Cap'n Potts gives it me back, he shan't have his cabin-boy. As long as he keeps my kitten, I'll keep *you!*"

"Who's to let him know?" I asked.

"You shall write him a letter," said she, "and I'll send it up by Octopus."

With that she set me down in the ship's saloon, a very glorious room indeed, with golden plate and jewelled goblets on the tables, and hangings of rich leather on the walls. I took off my diving-suit, pulled out my notebook and pencil, and scribbled a note to Cap'n Potts. This was it:

Dear Cap'n Potts,
The Queen of the Catfish wants her Kittenfish, which is the green kitten we've got aboard the Rocking-horse, and she's going to keep me till she gets it, so if you want me back send down the Kitten by Octopus, but if you'd rather have the Kitten than me, don't bother.
I hope you are well, as this leaves me.
Yours obediently, Jim.

Just as I scribbled "Jim," the Queen of the Catfish looked up and said, "Is your letter done? The Octopus is ready to start."

"Here's the letter, ma'am-your-majesty," said I, "but I'm afraid the pencil won't stand salt water."

"We'll put it in a shell to keep it dry," said the Queen of the Catfish. The saloon was littered with junk of all sorts, and she picked out a big spotted shell with a mouth like a letter-box. Then she posted my letter in the shell, gave it to the Octopus and he went aloft.

I wondered a bit whether Cap'n Potts would rather keep the Kitten than have me back again. I would in his place, and I made ready to stay under the sea for the rest of my life. It wasn't a bad place to stay in, but I preferred the *Rocking-horse*. So when the Octopus came down again with the Kitten in its tentacle, I felt quite light-hearted.

It was a pretty sight to see the little green Kitten leap into its mother's fins, sea-mewing with pleasure; and the Queen of the Catfish was so pleased to see it that she turned from snarly to smiley.

"Get into your diving-suit, Jim," she said, "and my respects to your Captain, and tell him next time he catches a Kittenfish he must throw it back, or there'll be trouble."

"There *was* trouble," said I, "what with hurricanes, icebergs, pirates and all."

"Those were my doing," said the Queen of the Catfish, "but from now on you shall have fair winds and smooth sailing. Here's your lobster-pot." With that she handed me my pot, and it was full to the brim with lobsters. "Nasty vicious things!" said she. "Always nipping my kittens when they get the chance. I'm glad to be rid of a few. Goodbye, Jim."

"Goodbye, ma'am-your-majesty," said I.

"Booby!" she said.

The Octopus took me in one tentacle, and the lobster-pot in another; the Kitten waved its paw at me, and the Queen of the Catfish kissed her fin, and up we went. In another moment I and the lobsters were put down safe and sound on the deck of the good ship *Rocking-horse*, and wasn't I glad! I'd never thought to see her more.

Cap'n Potts was sorry to lose the Kitten, but when he saw the lobsters he said, "Well done, my lad; you're a first-class cabin-boy, *you* are!" Then the wind began to blow, and the sails began to fill, and the *Rocking-horse* was well under way when we all sat down to hot lobsters for tea.

And now see here what I've got in my pocket. It's the very shell I posted my letter in. I found it lying about the deck a few days later, and I've kept it ever since. It's a good shell and a pretty shell. Put it to your ear, and you'll hear the sea in it. But don't go putting it to your kitten's ear, or she might turn green — and then there *would* be trouble.

O'er Seas That Have No Beaches

Mervyn Peake

O'er seas that have no beaches
To end their waves upon,
I floated with twelve peaches,
A sofa and a swan.

The blunt waves crashed above us
The sharp waves burst around,
There was no one to love us,
No hope of being found —

Where, on the notched horizon
So endlessly a-drip,
I saw all of a sudden
No sign of any ship.

Jonah and the Whale and the Cod-Liver Oil

Miloš Macourek

Translated by Marie Burg

There was once a little boy called Jonah, who wanted to be a policeman on traffic duty. But policemen on traffic duty must be very tough so that they don't suffer from the bitter cold in winter, and Jonah was such a delicate little thing — partly because he wouldn't eat fish.

When he scratched his thumb and blew on it to soothe it, he coughed so much that Dad had to run to the telephone and dial 12345, and Doctor Dale came and gave Jonah some drops.

Or, when Jonah looked at a picture book and turned the pages a little too fast, the draft gave him such a cold that Dad had to run to the telephone and dial 12345, and Doctor Dale came and gave Jonah some powder.

Now one day, just as Jonah was going out with Mum and Dad to see Granny, Aunt Clotilda arrived and brought Jonah some peppermints as a going-away present. Of course, this was a silly thing to do and Aunt Clotilda ought to have had more sense. She ought to have bought a different kind of sweet — jelly babies, for

Jonah and the Whale and the Cod-Liver Oil

Miloš Macourek

Translated by Marie Burg

There was once a little boy called Jonah, who wanted to be a policeman on traffic duty. But policemen on traffic duty must be very tough so that they don't suffer from the bitter cold in winter, and Jonah was such a delicate little thing — partly because he wouldn't eat fish.

When he scratched his thumb and blew on it to soothe it, he coughed so much that Dad had to run to the telephone and dial 12345, and Doctor Dale came and gave Jonah some drops.

Or, when Jonah looked at a picture book and turned the pages a little too fast, the draft gave him such a cold that Dad had to run to the telephone and dial 12345, and Doctor Dale came and gave Jonah some powder.

Now one day, just as Jonah was going out with Mum and Dad to see Granny, Aunt Clotilda arrived and brought Jonah some peppermints as a going-away present. Of course, this was a silly thing to do and Aunt Clotilda ought to have had more sense. She ought to have bought a different kind of sweet — jelly babies, for example — but she was thinking of goodness knows what, and so she bought peppermints and gave them to Jonah.

Well, poor little Jonah swallowed one of the peppermints. As he swallowed, the peppermint scorched his mouth, nearly lifting the roof off it, and it made his ears buzz too; and when he opened his mouth, all the newspapers and old cinema tickets flew all over the place, the tablecloth was fluttering, and Aunt Clotilda and Mum had to hold down their skirts.

It's no laughing matter, having such a gale blowing down your throat and Jonah, of course, fell ill with a sore throat. That's even worse than having a cold or a cough, so Dad ran to the telephone faster than usual. He meant to dial 12345 but, because he was thinking that it would be a long time before they could go to Granny's, he dialed 12346 instead. When the doorbell rang a few minutes later, it wasn't Doctor Dale who had come but Mr Whale.

"What can I do for you?" asked Dad.

"You rang me up," said Mr Whale. "My number is 12346."

"That's a mistake," said Dad, "I must have dialed the wrong number. I called Doctor Dale, because Jonah has a sore throat."

"That's all right," said Mr Whale. "As it happens, I do know a thing or two about medicine," and he went straight into the room.

"Good day, Jonah," said Mr Whale. "Open your mouth and say *ah* so that I can see what's the matter with you."

Jonah said *ah*, and Mr Whale looked at his throat and said: "It's flu. You'll have to gargle thoroughly."

But Aunt Clotilda wasn't satisfied. She took Dad into the hall and said: "We can't have Jonah treated by any old whale. What if he doesn't know anything about flu?"

She's right, thought Dad, there might be nasty complications. So he went back in the room and asked: "How can you tell it's flu? After all, you aren't a doctor, you're just an ordinary whale."

"And how can you tell that I don't know what I'm talking about," asked Mr Whale, "seeing as you're just an ordinary dad? As it happens, I do know what I'm talking about, because when I was small, I was a weak little thing and had flu myself from time to time. These days, of course, I don't know what it means to be ill. That's because I've grown tough in the Arctic Sea and I've been eating plenty of fish and cod-liver oil. Just look at me now! You see? I'm thirty-nine meters long. Jonah must gargle, and then we'll see."

"Hm," said Dad, "perhaps you're right. Jonah must gargle."

The trouble with Jonah was that he didn't know how to gargle. Mr Whale wanted to show him how to do it, but he had rather a large mouth. So he tried to gargle with the soap and the towel, the telephone and the little bed, but he couldn't manage it. Instead, he swallowed the lot, even the cooker and the saucepan and the radio, and the book of fairy-tales as well. In the end, he managed to gargle and so did Jonah, and they gargled together until Jonah was well again.

"Jonah is well again," said Mum and Dad and Aunt Clotilda to Mr Whale. "Thank you very much indeed.

You can go home now, we're off to Granny's."

"Hang on, hang on!" said Mr Whale. "You may *think* that Jonah is well, but he's not tough enough yet, because he doesn't eat fish or cod-liver oil."

"Hm," said Dad, "perhaps you're right. Jonah must be toughened up. If you can spare the time, stop here with him. We're going to stay with Granny, and when Jonah is tougher you can join us there. Cheerio, then."

"Cheerio," said Mr Whale. And he poured cold water into the bowl and called Jonah.

"Jonah, we're going to toughen you up. Wash your neck properly with the sponge, and your ears, and all the rest too."

"Brrr!" said Jonah to himself. "This water's like ice. I'm not going to wash myself in that!" And he took the sponge, and mopped up all the water in the bowl with it.

"I can't wash myself," he said to Mr Whale. "The bowl's quite empty."

That's strange, thought Mr Whale. Where could all the water have gone to? And he poured fresh water into the bowl.

Jonah took the sponge, mopped up all the water in the bowl with it, and said: "Look, I can't wash myself, because there's no water."

Am I going mad? thought Mr Whale. How is it that the water keeps disappearing? And he poured water into the bowl once more.

And once more Jonah took the sponge, and once more he mopped up all the water in the bowl with it. By now the sponge was getting heavy, because there was as much water in it as there is in a pond.

"Where is all that water going to?" said Mr Whale to himself. And he poured water into the bowl again and again. And this went on until Mr Whale was quite worn out.

"I must have a rest now," he said to Jonah. "Let's leave it for the time being." And he sat down in the chair, where the sponge lay full of water.

In a second the whole place was flooded, in a second there was a sea of water all around them, and in the sea swam Mr Whale, his mouth wide open in astonishment, and in his mouth sat Jonah, shouting: "All aboard!"

"That's done it," said Mr Whale. "Now we're really swimming in an arctic sea. Come inside so that you don't catch cold. You aren't toughened up yet." He shut his mouth and Jonah was inside him.

Fortunately, Jonah didn't get on so badly inside Mr Whale. In his stomach he found all sorts of things — a bed, a radio, a fairy-tale book, soap, and a towel — so that he felt quite at home. He switched on a torch, lay down on the bed, and read fairy-tales.

As he was reading, the telephone rang. It was Mr Whale, who asked: "Aren't you hungry? There's some fish and cod-liver oil in the fridge. Help yourself!"

"No thanks," said Jonah, "I don't fancy eating that."

"All right," said Mr Whale, "just help yourself when you're hungry. Go to sleep now, and in the morning I'll teach you how to swim."

True enough, the next morning the whale opened his mouth and sank to the bottom, and soon he was filled with water. "Brrr!" cried Jonah. "The water's cold!"

So he dried himself with the towel and, to get warm, he did some exercises to the music on the radio. And, because he was hungry, he ate some fish and cod-liver oil. After a few days he even liked it, and he had got used to the cold water. In fact, he even went to have a shower upstairs, on Mr Whale's head.

And so he became a quite different little fellow: he'd grown by a head and he weighed twice as much as before, he wasn't worried by even the coldest wind, and because he was eating fish his bones were like the phosphor which shines in the sea.

"Do you know what, Jonah?" said Mr Whale one day. "We're going to swim to your Granny's. I think you're ready for it now."

So they swam to Granny's house. And when they arrived, everyone was amazed to see them.

"That can't be Jonah, our delicate little boy," said Granny and Mum and Dad and Aunt Clotilda.

"It is me!" said Jonah. "I'm not a delicate little boy any more."

"I'd like to give you some of my peppermints for a welcome-home present," said Aunt Clotilda, "but you know what happened last time."

"Huh!" said Jonah, and gobbled up five bags of peppermints at one go. And Aunt Clotilda was flying in the air for a fortnight!

Jonah said goodbye to Mr Whale and thanked him, and he did become a policeman on traffic duty. He never suffered from the cold, not even during the coldest of frosts, and at night he shone like a neon sign, so that all the drivers were very grateful to him, especially when it was foggy. They were very fond of him, they knew him by name, and they'd say:

"You're a shiner, Jonah!"

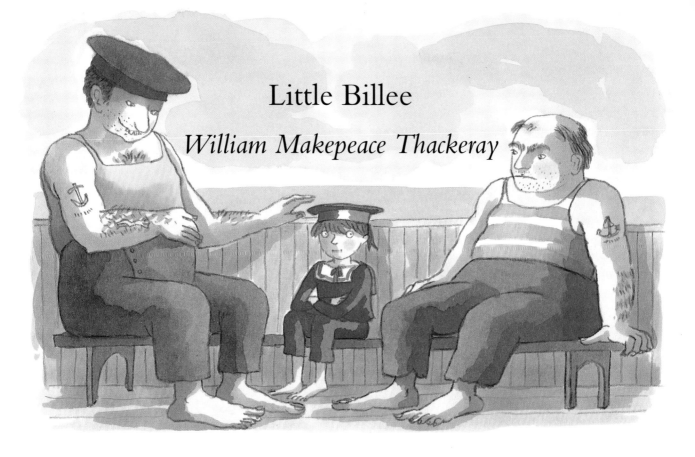

Little Billee

William Makepeace Thackeray

There were three sailors of Bristol city
    Who took a boat and went to sea.
But first with beef and captain's biscuits
    And pickled pork they loaded she.

There was gorging Jack and guzzling Jimmy,
    And the youngest he was little Billee.
Now when they got as far as the Equator
    They's nothing left but one split pea.

Says gorging Jack to guzzling Jimmy,
    "I am extremely hungaree."
To gorging Jack says guzzling Jimmy,
    "We've nothing left, us must eat we."

Says gorging Jack to guzzling Jimmy,
　　"With one another we shouldn't agree!
There's little Bill, he's young and tender,
　　We're old and tough, so let's eat he.

"Oh! Billy, we're going to kill and eat you,
　　So undo the button of your chemie."
When Bill received this information
　　He used his pocket handkerchie.

"First let me say my catechism,
　　Which my poor mammy taught to me."
"Make haste, make haste," says guzzling Jimmy,
　　While Jack pulled out his snickersee.

So Billy went up to the main-top gallant mast,
   And down he fell on bended knee.
He scarce had come to the twelfth commandment
   When up he jumps. "There's land I see:

"Jerusalem and Madagascar,
   And North and South Amerikee:
There's the British flag a-riding at anchor,
   With Admiral Napier, K.C.B."

So when they got aboard of the Admiral's
   He hanged fat Jack and flogged Jimmee:
But as for little Bill, he made him
   The Captain of a Seventy-three.

A Sea Story

Richard Hughes

There was once a little boy who ran away to sea, and was lucky enough to get a whole ship to himself. She was a large sailing ship; but the little boy knew all about sails, and could manage her alone.

For some years he sailed about from island to island, chiefly visiting the parrots who lived on them and teaching them English. Whenever he landed on an island, too, he used to spend a lot of time climbing the coconut palms (because these were tropical islands, with coconut palms and mangoes, and parrots and monkeys, and coral reefs and a bright sunny blue sea). When he was tired of one island he got back into his large ship and sailed to the next.

But after several years of lovely weather, one day the weather began to get bad. The sky grew cloudy and the wind began to blow too hard. Big gray clouds came rolling up from the edge of the sea, and went tumbling by overhead as fast as race-horses; and the wind grew stronger every minute. It grew stronger so fast that the little boy had no time to change his fine-weather sails for his

bad-weather sails, and so all his fine-weather sails got blown away and torn to ribbons.

The little boy soon guessed that this was no ordinary storm, but a storm got up against him by some enemy who knew how to do wicked magic; so he thought he had better go down into the cabin and shut the door, and watch to see what happened.

Meanwhile the waves had got huge, and were tossing the ship about so much that he had to hold on to the arms of the cabin sofa or he would have been rolled off onto the floor! So he sat there, wishing for the first time that he was not quite alone on so big a ship.

"*Ha, ha! But you are not alone!*" said a hard, wicked voice suddenly behind him.

The little boy jumped up in a fright, and then saw a parrot sitting on the cabin shelf.

"Oh, good gracious!" said the little boy. "You did give me a fright! I thought you might be the witch who has made the storm, and, after all, you are only a parrot off one of the islands!"

The parrot put her head on one side and scratched her ear

with her claw, and gave a long, wicked laugh again.

"I am only a parrot, am I?" she said in a low, witch-like voice; and then to his surprise the little boy saw the parrot begin to change. She spread out her wings, and they changed into long, skinny arms; and her beak changed into a great hooked nose, and her bright feathers into just the sort of gaudy, tattered rags that a witch would wear.

"I *am* only a parrot, am I?" she said, jumping down off the shelf on to the cabin floor.

Now, when the little boy saw it was really a witch, he started to edge his way toward the cabin stove, because by the fire he kept his magic poker. It was one of the few things that he had brought with him when he ran away from home, because he knew it would come in useful some day, because he knew it hated witches and was far the best thing to fight them with.

The witch watched him edging along toward the stove.

"I know what you are after," she said. "Your magic poker!" But, strange to say, she didn't try to stop him.

So the little boy gave a quick look at the stove; and then he saw why she hadn't tried to stop him. The magic poker was gone!

"Ha, ha!" said the witch. "You don't think I'd come into the cabin with *that* there, do you? I've put it in a safe place, where *you* won't find it, young man!"

"Have you?" said a ringing voice from the cabin stairs; and to the surprise of them both, there came the poker hopping downstairs as fast as it could (being only one-legged). "You thought you had fastened me up safe, didn't you? But I know better magic than you!" And before you could say "knife" the witch was yowling and running around the cabin, and the poker banging and bumping her wherever she went.

"Good!" said the little boy, full of pleasure. "Hit her hard, drive her out!"

And that is just what the good little poker presently did. It gave her a couple of good bangs on the head, and then chased her up the cabin stairs and out onto the deck, thumping her all the time. Three times round the deck they ran; and at last the witch jumped over the ship's side into the sea.

Now, witches, you know, cannot drown; if they fall into the water they float, and I have no doubt that the witch this time did not mind in the least jumping overboard, because she thought she would float away to safety. But she had not reckoned with that magic poker. His head was small, but his magic was strong, and he thought of everything; so before he came down to the cabin he had wrought a wonderful change in the sea. He had changed all the waves into sea-dragons. These dragons were as good as they were beautiful; and the moment they saw the witch, they opened up their foaming white jaws and swallowed her up, chomping her to bits in their teeth.

When the little boy looked over the side and saw there was now no sea at all, but it was all turned to dragons who rocked

the ship in their heaving about just like the sea did, and rolled their gleaming green sides and white crests almost like waves, he was astonished and a bit worried. For it was plain to him that there was now no sea at all. The ship was supported on nothing but dragons; and though he knew very well how to sail his ship on the sea, sailing his ship on dragons was something totally strange to him.

But things didn't stay like that for long. For now they had swallowed the witch, the dragons had nothing left to stay for; and they began to flounder away in different directions. When they did that, of course, the ship went down and down, until presently they were all gone, and she was resting actually on the sandy bottom of what had been the sea, but now was quite dry.

The little boy was very excited at seeing the wonderful things on the bottom of the sea left all bare like this. Among them he saw the wreck of an old Spanish galleon, which had sunk long ago. It was covered with barnacles and seaweed, now already beginning to dry in the sun. Immediately the little boy climbed down a rope over the side of his own ship and ran across the sand to explore the wreck, and sure enough, it was full nearly to the deck with chests of gold and jewels.

So the little boy carried as many of them as he could

(though they were frightfully heavy) across from the wrecked galleon to his own ship, and stowed them in the hold.

But when he had done that, he began to be very worried again. It was nice to have his ship loaded with treasure; but what was he to do next?

For his ship, like the wreck, was high and dry on the sand, on what had been the bottom of the sea; and how was he ever to sail away, with no sea at all to sail it on?

So he wandered back again to the galleon, and went on exploring her; and presently he found a curious hammer hanging from a peg on the wall. There was magic-looking writing on it. The little boy could read that kind of writing, and what it said was this:

When the waters flee
Strike the bottom thrice with me.

So the little boy took the hammer off the peg, and jumped down out of the wreck and struck a rock once with the hammer. Nothing happened; so he struck the rock a second time. Still nothing happened.

"It *did* say 'thrice'," said the little boy to himself, "and 'thrice' means three times, so I will try again."

So he then struck the rock a third time. Suddenly fountains started appearing out of the sand

in all directions. Water began gushing up out of the ground, as if all the water-pipes in the world had burst; and in almost no time the little boy was up to his ankles. There was no time to be lost, so he began to run for his ship; but before he got anywhere near her, the water was up to his waist. Now it is very difficult to run in water up to one's waist; but he did his best, and just before the water reached his chin he managed to catch hold of the rope which he had left dangling over the side, and so to haul himself up on board.

Meanwhile the water roared and swirled around, and rose faster and faster, and before very long he felt his ship begin to rock; and presently the water lifted her clear of the bottom, and she floated on top of the sea once more.

When his ship was afloat again, the little boy felt he had had enough of adventures for a time; so he brought out his spare sails, and rigged them in place of the ones which had blown away, and sailed back to the shores of his own home; and there he landed at last with all the gold and jewels he had got from the wreck of the Spanish galleon.

But he was even more careful to carry his magic poker safely ashore than he was with the gold and silver, for a poker which could thump witches like that on its own was not a poker to lose carelessly! It was worth more than all the gold and silver on the whole of the ocean bottom.

Little Fan

James Reeves

"I don't like the look of little Fan, mother,
    I don't like her looks a little bit.
Her face — well, it's not exactly different,
    But there's something wrong with it.

"She went down to the sea-shore yesterday,
    And she talked to somebody there,
Now she won't do anything but sit
    And comb out her yellowy hair.

"Her eyes are shiny and she sings, mother,
    Like nobody ever sang before.
Perhaps they gave her something queer to eat,
    Down by the rocks on the shore.

"Speak to me, speak, little Fan dear,
    Aren't you feeling very well?
Where have you been and what are you singing,
    And what's that seaweedy smell?

"Where did you get that shiny comb, love,
    And those pretty coral beads so red?
Yesterday you had two legs, I'm certain,
    But now there's something else instead.

"I don't like the looks of little Fan, mother,
    You'd best go and close the door.
Watch now, or she'll be gone for ever
    To the rocks by the brown sandy shore."

Prince Crab

A Venetian Folk Tale

Retold by Laura Cecil

There was once a beautiful princess who lived in a palace overlooking the sea.

One day she heard a great commotion coming from the palace kitchen, so she ran down to see what was happening. A ragged fisherman was shouting at the palace cook as they tried to push a giant crab, perched on a tiny cart, into the kitchen. The poor creature was stuck on its back, with its long legs waving helplessly in the air.

"How could you be so cruel to such a splendid creature?" cried the princess.

"My family is starving," the fisherman said. "I must sell this beast or they will die."

The princess was even more horrified when the cook told her it was just what he wanted for the banquet that night. So she immediately ran to her father and asked him to buy the crab for her, as she was determined to save it. Her father could refuse her nothing and the fisherman was soon on his way with a bag of gold.

From then on the crab lived a happy life in a large ornamental pond in the middle of the palace garden. He had a glowing red shell with huge claws tipped with black, and the princess was fascinated by him. She loved to watch as he swam in and out of the shells and waving weeds at the bottom of the pond. Several times a day she would visit him and throw him the best food she could find. Sometimes, when she played her harp beside the pond, the crab seemed to enjoy the music and

would swing his great claws in time to the melodies. He seemed to understand when she spoke to him, and often he would come to the surface to greet her. But after a while, she learned that he would never appear between noon and three o'clock. At first she thought it must be his time for sleeping. But it began to puzzle her, for although he was so large, try as she might, she could never see where he went.

One day she came to the pond at noon, determined to find out where he had gone. She leaned further and further over the edge, craning her neck to see whether he was under a rock at the bottom, when SPLASH! in she toppled. She just had time to hold her breath before she found herself whirled down and down into an underground passage that led to a cavern far out under the ocean. When the princess emerged from the water she saw she was in a splendid underwater palace hung with tapestries made of shells and many-colored seaweeds.

Then she heard voices, so she quickly hid herself behind the hangings. To her amazement, in came her crab with a seawitch riding on his huge back. The seawitch had a cruel face, and in her long seaweedy hair she wore a purple flower. She dismounted, tapped the crab shell with her wand, whereupon it opened and out stepped a handsome young man. He and the seawitch sat down to eat a meal. While their backs were turned, the princess crept out and slipped into the crab shell, swiftly pulling the top half down over herself. Then, when it was nearly three o'clock, the young man said goodbye to the seawitch and stepped back into his shell. He was amazed when he found the princess there already, but he quickly signed to her to make no noise, so she would not be found out. Meanwhile, the seawitch tapped the top of the shell and the crab set out on his journey up the secret tunnel to the king's pond.

From inside the shell the young man worked the crab's hind limbs and they moved swiftly through the water. As they went he told the princess his sad story:

"I was once a powerful prince, but the wicked seawitch has enchanted me. She wants me all for herself, so she has forced me to live in this crab shell."

"But how can you break such a cruel spell?" asked the princess.

"Only a maiden who is willing to risk her life for me can do this," said the prince.

"I will," answered the princess, who loved him already, "but how can I save you?"

"The seawitch loves a certain magic song and you must sit by the sea and play it on your harp until she appears. She will beg you to play it again, but you must refuse unless she promises to give you the flower she always wears in her hair. The seawitch will be so enthralled by the music, she will agree immediately. Once you have the flower the enchantment will be broken because the flower is my life. But you must take care, although the seawitch will have to keep her promise, she will try to cheat you."

Then the prince sang the magic song and the princess knew it by the time they reached the surface of the palace pond.

"Alas, you are free to go but I am trapped in this hateful shell," sighed the young man as he tapped the inside of the shell and the princess climbed out. Humming the magic song under her breath, she went into the palace to find her harp. All the rest of the day she played it over and over again until she knew the melody perfectly.

"Click your claws together if this sounds right, my dearest crab," she said when she came to the pond that night. When she had finished playing she heard a loud click from his immense claws, which showed just above the surface of the water.

The next day she went down to the seashore and sat on a high rock to play the magic song. Sure enough, the seawitch appeared out of the waves as soon as she had finished. The purple flower gleamed in her hair.

"You must play that song again — you must, you must!" pleaded the seawitch.

"Not unless you promise to give me the flower in your hair."

"I promise," said the seawitch.

But when the princess finished playing, the seawitch screamed, "There, take it!" and flung the flower as far as she could into the rough sea. Unafraid, the princess dived off her rock and swam strongly after the flower. Just as she was about to reach it, the witch sent a huge wave which sucked the princess underwater, half drowning her. Suddenly, she felt the

strong shell of the crab lifting her up out of the sea. She stretched out and grasped the flower. The seawitch plunged under the surf with an angry wail, defeated.

"You have saved me!" cried the crab as he carried the princess safely back toward the land. As they went he told her he must first return to his own country, but he would come to the princess's kingdom soon and ask her father for her hand in marriage. When they reached the shore, he climbed out of his shell for the last time and they watched as the waves swept it out to sea.

The princess's father was surprised and delighted when the rich young prince arrived with a fine retinue to ask to marry his daughter. The princess agreed immediately and there was a splendid wedding. The prince and princess lived happily ever after, but the king always wondered why the prince did not want to live in the palace by the sea. He could not understand why the young man disliked swimming so much, especially going underwater.

Seal Lullaby

Rudyard Kipling

Oh! hush thee, my baby, the night is behind us,
And black are the waters that sparkled so grccn.
The moon, o'er the combers, looks downward to find us
At rest in the hollows that rustle between.
Where billow meets billow, there soft be thy pillow;
Ah, weary wee flipperling, curl at thy ease!
The storm shall not wake thee, nor sharks overtake thee,
Asleep in the arms of the slow-swinging seas.